WALT DISNEY'S
DONALD DUCK
ADVENTURES

TAKE-ALONG COMIC

GEMSTONE PUBLISHING
TIMONIUM, MARYLAND

STEPHEN A. GEPPI
*President/Publisher and
Chief Executive Officer*

JOHN K. SNYDER JR.
Chief Administrative Officer

STAFF

LEONARD (JOHN) CLARK
Editor-in-Chief

GARY LEACH
Associate Editor

SUE KOLBERG
Assistant Editor

TRAVIS SEITLER
Art Director

SUSAN DAIGLE-LEACH
Production Associate

MELISSA BOWERSOX
Director-Creative Projects

• **IN THIS ISSUE** •

Cover illustration by **William Van Horn** Cover color by **Gary Leach**
Original story color by **Egmont**
Lettering and color modifications by
Susan Daigle-Leach and **Gary Leach**

ADVERTISING/ MARKETING

J.C. VAUGHN
Executive Editor

ARNOLD T. BLUMBERG
Editor

BRENDA BUSICK
Creative Director

JAMIE DAVID
Director of Marketing

SARA ORTT
Assistant Executive Liaison
Toll Free
(888) 375-9800 Ext. 410
ads@gemstonepub.com

MARK HUESMAN
Production Assistant

MIKE WILBUR
Shipping Manager

WALT DISNEY'S DONALD DUCK ADVENTURES 11
Take-Along Comic
March, 2005

Published by
Gemstone Publishing

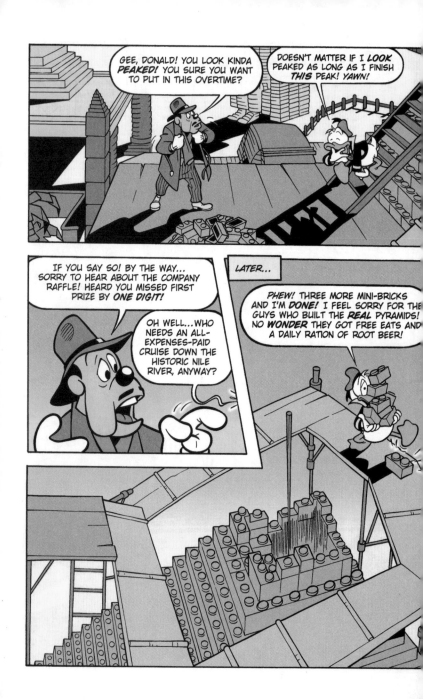

AS FOR THE *NEXT* WONDER OF THE WORLD, *I* WONDER IF THEY CAN FIND *ANOTHER* SUCKER! I'M NOT DOING THE "FALL OF ROME"! HUH...?

LOOK OUT BELOOOW!

CRASH

SMASH

GROAN!

WHAT A *CATASTROPHE*! A *DISASTROUS DISASTER*! A *CALAMITOUS CALAMITY*! A *TRAGIC TRAGEDY*! EH...?

BRRING

DONALD? PARK MANAGER HERE! HOW'S THE WORK GOING?

UH...JUST *SMASHING*! GULP!

ANY TWISTS AND TURNS LATER...

PLEASE LET THIS BE AN EXIT...

WOW!

THEY SURE WRAPPED A LOT OF BANDAGES AROUND THIS POOR DUDE! MUST HAVE BEEN A GNARLY ACCIDENT!

CREAK

WHO DARES DISTURB THE TOMB OF TOOT?

ULP!

THE CURSE OF TOOT BE UPON YOU, DEFILER!

MU-MUMMY!

GROAN...

ANYWAY, I'D LOVE TO STOP AND CHAT, BUT I'M IN THE MIDDLE OF BEING CHASED BY TWO BANDAGED BADDIES...

EXCUSE ME, BUT... WHO ARE YOU? AND WHAT ARE YOU DOING HERE? THIS IS A RESTRICTED AREA!

ME? I WAS SIGHTSEEING WITH A TOUR GROUP AND I GOT LOST!

WELL...THIS PYRAMID *IS* PRETTY TWISTY-TURNY! EVEN *I* GET LOST SOMETIMES!

I DON'T THINK YOU GET MY DRIFT! THAT *BEDSHEET MODEL* IS GONNA TEAR ME *LIMB* FROM *FEATHER*!

OH, THOSE AREN'T *REAL* MUMMIES! THEY'RE JUST *ROBOTS* LINKED TO AN ALARM SYSTEM TO CHASE OFF GRAVEROBBERS!

WE'VE LOST SO MANY HISTORICAL ARTIFACTS TO THIEVES LATELY, WE HAD TO COME UP WITH *SOME* WAY TO DISSUADE THEM!

SORRY...THE NAME'S DEZZI DIGGER, *CHIEF ARCHAEOLOGIST* OF THIS REGION!

DONALD DUCK! AND THAT'S AN IMPRESSIVE CREDENTIAL!

THANKS!

THIS ROOM IS THE ANTECHAMBER TO THE BURIAL TOMB OF TOOT III! HE WAS RENOWNED FOR DESIGNING PYRAMIDS WITH *SECRET PASSAGES* AND *TRAPS* TO FOIL ROBBERS!

SEE THIS SARCOPHAGUS CAMOUFLAGING A SECRET ENTRANCE? ONE OF HIS SIGNATURE TRICKS!

AND THERE'S THE *MAN WITH THE PLAN!*

THE *BIG-AND-TALL* TYPE, EH? WHAT'S WITH THE HOLE IN HIS HEAD?

*SIGH...THAT HOLE ONCE HELD A GLEAMING *BLACK JADE* KNOWN AS THE "EYE OF RA!" IT WAS STOLEN DURING THE EXCAVATION BY WORKERS WHO PROBABLY HAD NO IDEA OF ITS VALUE!*

THE EYE IS A *PRICELESS ARTIFACT!* IT HOLDS THE *KEY* TO THE *GREAT PYRAMID*, WHICH HOUSES THE STILL UNDISCOVERED TOMB OF *TUTTI-FRUITTI*, THE *GREATEST* OF ALL THE *PHARAOHS!*

DON'T WORRY! YOU CAN TAKE A *SHIP* TO YOUR SHIP!

HUH?

VOILA! THE *SHIP OF THE DESERT!*

UMM...HOW DO I STEER THIS CRITTER?

NO NEED! SHE'LL TAKE YOU DIRECTLY TO THE MAIN BAZAAR, ONLY A SHORT WALK FROM THE DOCKS! AND IF YOU GET A CHANCE...

...BEFORE YOU SET SAIL, DROP BY THE MUSEUM AND I'LL SHOW YOU AROUND.

AND BE CAREFUL SHOPPING AT THE BAZAAR! SOME OF THOSE TRADERS ARE *CON ARTISTS!*

SO LONG!

UH-OH! I'M FEELING *SEASICK* ALREADY!

AH! HONORED SUCKER...I MEAN, *GUEST!* WELCOME TO MY HUMBLE EMPORIUM!

NICE DECOR! NOW, WHICH WAY TO...

I SEE YOU HAVE BEEN THE VICTIM OF *UNSCRUPULOUS MERCHANTS!* ALLOW ME!

WELL, I *DO* THINK THEY OVERCHARGED ME A *LITTLE*...

DON'T BURDEN YOURSELF WITH SUCH RUBBISH!

UH... RIGHT!

JUNK

INSTEAD, ALLOW ME TO OFFER YOU *GENUINE RELICS* OF THE PHARAOHS!

LIKE THESE *AUTHENTIC MUMMY PARTS!*

MUMMY PARTS?

GOOD NEWS, SLYMIR! THE EYE OF RA IS OURS AT LAST! GO AND FETCH IT!

WITH GREAT PLEASURE!

WAIT A SEC...

DID YOU JUST TELL HIM TO FETCH THE EYE OF RA...?

WHAT'S IT TO YOU?

SLAM!

WELL, *UH*... JUST THAT YOU WERE *HOLDING* IT IN YOUR *HAND* JUST NOW AND SELLING IT TO ME!

AH! YOU MEAN *THIS* EYE!

BUT OF COURSE! THERE! IT'S ALL YOURS! NOW IF YOU'LL EXCUSE ME...

...WE'RE *CLOSED!*

SLAM!

THAT CUTE ARCHEOLOGIST WILL *JUMP FOR JOY* WHEN SHE SETS HER PEEPERS ON THIS! MAYBE SHE'LL EVEN GO OUT FOR A SODA WITH ME!

"DEZZI DIGGER, PLEASE..."

YOU'LL FIND HER DOWN THE HALL, IN THE MAIN EXHIBIT ROOM.

CAIRO MUSEUM

IT'S NOT MUCH, BUT IT'S FINISHED!

AHEM!

MR. DUCK! WHAT A PLEASANT SURPRISE! BUT... WHY ARE YOU DRESSED LIKE THAT?

OH, YOU KNOW..."WHEN IN ROME, DO AS THE ROMANS DO!" SO WHEN IN EGYPT...WELL, YOU GET THE IDEA!

AM I DISTURBING YOU?

OH, NO. I'VE JUST FINISHED A SMALL DISPLAY ABOUT TUTTIFRUITTI'S DYNASTY! IF ONLY WE COULD FIND HIS TOMB...

IF YOU HAD THE *EYE OF RA*, YOU'D KNOW WHERE TO LOOK, RIGHT?

THE GREAT PYRAMID

INDEED! IF *ONLY!*

WELL, *LOOK NO FURTHER!* BECAUSE I'VE *DUG IT UP,* SO TO SPEAK!

AREN'T YOU GONNA CONGRATULATE ME ON MY ARCHEOPOTOMUS...*UH* ...ARCHEOGEODE...*UH*... *DETECTIVE* SKILLS?

OH! WELL, THAT IS...I MEAN, YOU SEE...

HAR! HAR! HAR!

HAR! HAR! THAT'S RICH! THAT'S REALLY RICH!

PLEASE, SULTAN! IT'S NOT THAT FUNNY!

HUH!?

FORGIVE ME...MMPH! MY NAME IS SULTAN! I ASSIST – GIGGLE – MS. DIGGER IN HER... MMPH...WORK! *HEH HEH HEH...*

BWA-HA-HA-HA-HA!

REALLY, SULTAN!

UH...WHAT'S SO FUNNY?

OH, I WILL! NOW THAT I'VE BEEN HUMILIATED IN FRONT OF A *SMART GIRL!* AND BEEN *CHEATED! RIDICULED! VILIFIED!* AND OTHER FUN THINGS!

FINE! I'M GONNA TEACH THAT SON OF A CAMEL A LESSON! WHEN I'M THROUGH WITH HIM HE'LL WISH HE RAN AN ICE-CUBE SHOP INSTEAD OF A...

"...JUNK PARLOR!"

WHERE THE DEVIL HAS THAT SLYMIR GOT TO?

HEY! WHAT'S THE BIG IDEA? CAN'T YOU SEE WE'RE CLOSED?

I'VE GOT A BONE TO PICK WITH YOU, MISTER! AND THIS ONE AIN'T *ANCIENT!*

LISTEN HERE, *SCORPION-FACE!* THIS EYE IS A *FRAUD!* GIMME MY *POUNDS* BACK OR I'LL POUND *YOU!*

REALLY? THEN FEEL FREE TO RAISE YOUR COMPLAINT WITH MY CUSTOMER SERVICE MANAGER!

OH, SHARKIR!

YUH! WHAT'S THE PROBLEM, BOSS?

THIS CUSTOMER APPEARS TO BE *DISSATISFIED!*

GULP!

GIVE ME MY EYE BACK, HAMBURGER-BREATH!

HOLD YOUR CAMELS, BAGGY-PANTS! *THIS* ONE'S *MINE!*

INFIDEL! HAND IT OVER LEST I FEED YOUR *INNARDS* TO THE *VULTURES!*

YIKES!

AHMED'S EMPORIUM

SUFFERING *SCARABS!* TALK ABOUT SHARP DEALING!

HERE IT IS!

SHEESH! THIS *BAZAAR* IS *BIZARRE!* I'VE BEEN ROBBED, CHEATED, MAULED, HUMILIATED, INSULTED AND THREATENED!

ALL I WANT IS TO FIND MY SHIP AND SNOOZE TILL I'M BACK IN THE LAND OF *LAWNS* AND *SQUARE BUILDINGS!*

SLAM!

AT *LAST!* BY THE GREAT SNAKES OF LUXOR, WE SHALL BE *WEALTHY!*

EH? WHAT'S *THIS?*

YOU *CROSS-EYED TOAD!* THIS IS ONE OF *MY FAKES!*

IMPOSSIBLE! I CHECKED IT OUT! AND IT HASN'T BEEN OUT OF MY HANDS EXCEPT...

YES? EXCEPT...

BY THE GREAT PYRAMIDS! EXCEPT WHEN I WAS KNOCKED OFF MY FEET BY THAT TOURIST WE FLEECED! HE MUST HAVE *SWITCHED EYES* ON ME!

HIM? *GREAT SUFFERING SPHINXES!* YOU IMBECILE! HE LEFT HERE WITH ONE OF MY FAKES! HE MUST HAVE *SWITCHED* THEM!

SHARKIR!

SHORTLY...

THESE STREETS ARE MORE *A-MAZING* THAN THAT TOMB! I'M *SURE* I'VE BEEN HERE BEFORE...

THERE HE IS! *GET HIM!*

YUH! I BREAKS HIM INTO TEENSY-WEENSY PIECES...

AIEEEE!

BOUNCE!

OOF!

THUMP!

THAT CAMEL'S GOT MORE *KICK* THAN MY *CAR'S* GOT *HORSEPOWER!*

RUH! SHARKIR WANT *PRETTY BLACK EYE!*

SO IT'S THE *EYE* THEY'RE AFTER? BUT WHEN I *TRIED* TO GIVE IT BACK, THEY DIDN'T WANT IT! AND NOW THAT THEY'VE *STOLEN* IT, WHY'RE THEY STILL CHASING ME!?

THIS OUTFIT'S A LOUSY DISGUISE! BESIDES, I'M TIRED OF LOOKING LIKE A *TENT WITH FEET.*

HUH?!

CLACK!

PHEW! WHAT A RELIEF! *ANOTHER* EYE! IF I GIVE THEM *THIS* ONE, MAYBE THEY'LL LAY OFFA ME!

SHARKIR! OVER HERE!

NEVER MIND! YOU NEW GIRLS ARE ALL THE SAME, AND I'VE NO TIME FOR SOB STORIES! PUT THIS ON!

A MASK! GOOD IDEA!

AHA!

HUH! I LIKES YOU! WANNA BE MY GIRLFRIEND?

"GIRLFRIEND?" *GULP!* OH, I'D LOVE TO! BUT RIGHT NOW, I HAVE TO *POWDER MY VEIL!*

STOP *GIVING HER THE EYE,* YOU FOOL! WE'VE GOT BUSINESS TO ATTEND TO!

NOPE! NO TOURISTS COMMITTING *FASHION CRIME* AROUND HERE!

YOU LADIES HAPPEN TO SEE A RUBE IN A YELLOW JALAVAH?

I DIDN'T GIVE HER *THE EYE,* BOSS! HONEST!

SHUT UP, HUMMUS-FOR-BRAINS! GET MOVING!

PHEW!

OKAY, GIRLS! DO YOUR STUFF!

GOODNESS! STOP OGLING THAT GREAT OAF! YOU'RE *ON!*

...*VERY* FAMILIAR!

WHISPER... WHISPER...

HMM!

FORGIVE ME, MY DEAR! URGENT BUSINESS! IF YOU NEED ME, YOU CAN REACH ME ON MY CELL!

ALL RIGHT!

YUH! I LIKE THE *SHORT* ONE!

HEAVENLY HIEROGLYPHICS! GET A GRIP! WE'VE GOT WORK TO DO!

YIKES! THE GOONS ARE *BACK!*

THIS OUTFIT'S GOT THEM FOOLED FOR NOW! BUT THEY MIGHT NOT FALL FOR IT MUCH LO...

...OOONGE-E-E-R-R-R!

OOOOOF!

HUH!?

SMASH!

HELLO, MY BEAUTY! NICE OF YOU TO JOIN US! MAY I BUY YOU A ROSE WATER?

GET YOUR GREASY HANDS OFFA ME, FALAFEL-FACE!

HA! RIGHT ON THE BUTTON! AND I *DON'T* MEAN THE *BELLY* BUTTON!

GASP!

SLAP!

DEZZI!

DONALD!

SUFFERING SPHINXES!

AM I GLAD TO SEE — *HUH?*

YOU LUNATIC! AFFRONTING OUR CUSTOMERS LIKE THIS! YOUR DANCING DAYS ARE *OVER!* YOU'RE *FIRED!*

YEAH? WELL YOU'RE *TOO LATE,* 'CAUSE *I QUIT!* SO STOP YOUR *BELLYACHING!*

REALLY? THEN WE CAN DISPENSE WITH *FORMALITIES!*

SO MUCH FOR A CLEAN EXIT...

DONALD!

WHAT'S GOING ON? WHY ARE YOU DRESSED AS A BELLYDANCER?

PHEW! AM I GLAD TO SEE YOU! A BUNCH OF KOOKS ARE CHASING ME THANKS TO THAT PHONY BALONEY EYE I BOUGHT!

I'D GIVE THEM *MY* EYE — THE ONE I FOUND IN MY NATIVE NIGHTGOWN, I MEAN — BUT THEY WANT MY *GIBLETS*, TOO!

WHY WOULD ANYONE BE SO UPSET OVER A *CHEAP IMITATION?*

SEARCH ME! I JUST WISH THEY'D LEAVE ME ALONE AND GO PLAY IN THE SAND!

GASP!

D-DONALD! *THIS* EYE IS THE *REAL THING!*

IT IS?

YES! WHICH EXPLAINS WHY YOU'RE BEING SO DOGGEDLY PURSUED! QUICK-MY CAR IS AROUND THE CORNER! LET'S GET OUT OF HERE BEFORE THEY TURN UP AGAIN!

I'LL HEAD FOR THE MUSEUM, AND ON THE WAY, I WANT YOU TO TELL ME THE...

VROOM!

"...WHOLE STORY!"

WELL, THAT'S QUITE A TALE! I DON'T QUITE FOLLOW ALL OF IT, BUT WHAT I GATHER IS THAT WE'VE FINALLY RUN INTO A BIT OF LUCK!

LUCK?

LUCK FOR THE *MUSEUM,* I MEAN! NOW THAT WE HAVE THE EYE, WE'LL BE THE FIRST TO LOCATE TUTTIFRUITTI'S TOMB IN THE GREAT PYRAMID BEFORE ANYONE RANSACKS IT!

BUT WHAT ABOUT *ME?* I'M STILL ON THAT SHIFTY SHOPKEEPER'S HIT LIST!

CAIRO

DON'T FRET! WE'LL SOON HAVE YOU BACK ON YOUR SHIP OUT OF HARM'S...

AH, SULTAN! I NEED YOU HERE AT THE MUSEUM, ASAP! IT'S ABOUT THE *EYE OF RA!* I CAN'T EXPLAIN ON THE PHONE, BUT HURRY! AND BRING THE *POLICE* WITH YOU!

THERE! EVERYTHING'S GOING TO BE FINE! NOW FOLLOW ME! I WANT TO SHOW YOU JUST WHY THE EYE...

"...IS SO VALUABLE!"

SEE HERE, ETCHED ON ITS SURFACE? IT HAS A PLAN OF THE GREAT PYRAMID — THE ENTRANCE, THE PASSAGEWAYS, THE TRAPS, AND THE LOCATION OF TUTTIFRUITTI'S TOMB—

WHAT THE DEVIL'S GOING ON?

678

WHAT'S THAT *CHUMP* DOING HERE IN THAT OUTFIT — THE *DANCE OF THE IGNORAMUS?*

I'M SO GLAD YOU'RE HERE! I'VE GOT *WONDERFUL NEWS!* DONALD HAS FOUND THE *EYE OF RA!* ISN'T THAT GREAT?

GASP! *THE EYE!*

GIVE ME THAT!

HEY!

WHAT ARE YOU DOING? I DON'T UNDERSTAND—

SHUT UP! WE'VE BEEN *SCOURING THE CITY* FOR THIS — *AND* THAT DONKEY-BRAINED FRIEND OF YOURS!

AHMED! GET IN HERE!

I'VE FOUND WHAT YOU INCOMPETENTS MANAGED TO MISLAY! NOW TRUSS THIS PAIR OF LOSERS IN BURIAL WRAPPINGS AND TOSS THEM IN A CASKET! WE'LL DUMP THEM OUTSIDE THE CITY!

EXPLAIN YOURSELF, SULTAN!

YUH! CAN I DO *BREAKING NOW*, BOSS?

I'M THAT ELUSIVE MASTERMIND BEHIND THE ROBBING OF THE TOMBS YOU'VE DISCOVERED! AND NOW I WILL PLUNDER THE *GREATEST ARCHEO-LOGICAL FIND OF THEM ALL!*

GASP! YOU MEAN...

YES, MY INNOCENT! IT'S BEEN *ME* ALL ALONG! YOU DON'T THINK I *TOIL* IN THIS *DUSTBOWL* FOR *LOVE*, DO YOU? NO, NO! I'M JUST TAKING ADVANTAGE OF YOUR DILIGENT RESEARCH TO LEAD MY BOYS TO *UNTOLD TREASURES!*

YOU FIEND! YOU'LL PAY FOR THIS!

IF YOU'RE EXPECTING THE *POLICE* TO ARRIVE, FORGET IT! NATURALLY I NEVER CALLED THEM! AND WHERE *YOU'RE* GOING, THERE AREN'T ANY PHONES! *BWA-HA-HA!*

NOW LET'S GET THIS BUSINESS WRAPPED UP!

SOON...

I'M SORRY, DONALD! THIS IS ALL MY FAULT!

THAT'S OKAY! AT LEAST WHATEVER HAPPENS, WE'RE ALREADY *PRE-BANDAGED!*

COMFY? *GOOD!*

WHOO! AND I THOUGHT MY CABIN ON THE CRUISE SHIP WAS CRAMPED!

SLAM!

UNDER THE SHINING MOON...

STOW THEM INSIDE! HURRY! THIS TOMB ISN'T ON THE PUBLIC RECORD YET, SO NO ONE WILL EVER FIND THEM!

YOU SEE, SHISH? I *TOLD* YOU IF WE TAILED THESE MUSEUM FOLK THEY WOULD LEAD US TO THEIR SECRET DIGS SOME DAY!

YOU WERE RIGHT, KEBAB! NOW LET'S HURRY AND OPEN HER UP TO SEE...

...WHAT *RICHES* AWAIT US!

CREEAK!

MMMFF!

AllEEEEEEE!

WAAH!

WHAT'S BITTEN *THOSE* TWO?

VERILY, THEY HAVE ANTS IN THEIR PANTS!

DON'T WORRY! WE'LL THINK OF SOMETHING!

HOLD IT!

YIKES!

PHEW! *THAT* WAS CLOSE! ONE OF TOOT'S FAMOUS TRAPS, LOOKS LIKE!

I'M NOT READY TO BE *SHISH-KA-DONALD* JUST YET! CONSIDERING ALL THESE BOOBY-TRAPS...

WHY DON'T WE JUST WAIT *OUTSIDE* FOR THOSE NO-GOODS?

ACTUALLY, THAT'S A GOOD IDEA! LET'S HEAD BACK TO THE—

RUMBLE!

SLAM!

OOPS! SO MUCH FOR GOOD IDEAS!

OUR BACKS ARE **REALLY** AGAINST THE WALL NOW!

AFRAID SO! UNLESS YOU'VE GOT A KNACK FOR **SNAKE CHARMING**, WE'RE...

...**FANG FOOD!** OH!

OOPS!

CRUMBLE!

WHAT A STROKE OF LUCK! A FAKE WALL! AND A WAY OUT!

WHEW! GLAD TO GIVE THOSE SLITHERY SNAPPERS THE SLIP!

NOW WHERE ARE WE?

LOOKS LIKE...

...*THAT'S* WHERE WE *CAME IN!* LET'S SEE WHAT'S AROUND THIS CORNER!

SHEESH! IT'S LIKE BEING LOST IN A *SWISS CHEESE!*

WE'VE FALLEN FOR THAT BOOB'S TRAPS TWICE, BUT OLD TOOT'S NOT GONNA CATCH ME NAPPING A THIRD TIME—

SHHHH!

COME ON! THIS LOOKS LIKE TUTTIFRUITTI'S CHAMBER! AND THERE'S SOMEONE IN THERE!

UM...ISN'T THAT A GOOD REASON TO HEAD THE OTHER WAY?

WE'RE *JUST IN TIME!*

REALLY? FOR WHAT?

CAREFUL, YOU FOOLS.

DON'T RISK DAMAGING THE CONTENTS!

WHAT ARE YOU DOING?

QUICK! TAKE OFF YOUR WRAPPINGS! I'VE GOT AN IDEA!

MOMENTS LATER...

NOW KEEP A HOLD OF THOSE WRAPPINGS AND I'LL GET THE BALL ROLLING!

SURE! WE'LL PROBABLY *NEED* THEM FOR *BANDAGES!*

WHAT A *COZY* SCENE! I HOPE YOU PLAN TO *DONATE* YOUR FIND TO THE MUSEUM!

YOU!?

DON'T JUST STAND THERE — *GET HER!*

MOVE IT, YOU OAFS!

LIKE A HERD OF HIPPOS!

...EVERYTHING MY-*WHUP!*

THUMP!

TIME TO *TIE UP* A FEW *LOOSE ENDS!*

ARGH!

AGH!

OW!

NNNNNGH!

I GUESS THAT *WRAPS IT UP!*

YEP! FOR SUCH A *SMOOTH TALKER,* HE LOOKS PRETTY *TONGUE-TIED!* NOW TO CALL IN...

"...THE COPS!"

THANK YOU, YOUNG MAN! YOU'RE A *HERO!*

DIRECTOR, MEET DONALD! HE FOUND THE *EYE* AND HELPED CATCH THOSE *ANTIQUITIES THIEVES!*

NOW THAT WE'VE CAPTURED THOSE CROOKS, RECOVERED TUTTI-FRUITTI'S SARCOPHAGUS, AND ENSURED THE SAFETY OF THE ARTIFACTS IN HIS TOMB, *I'D* LIKE TO SEE THE FAMOUS BURIAL CHAMBER!

COME RIGHT THIS WAY!

CAIRO MUSEUM

WONDERFUL! STUPENDOUS! NOT ONLY WILL THIS DISCOVERY ENHANCE OUR UNDERSTANDING OF THE PERIOD, IT'LL ATTRACT LOTS OF TOURISTS, RAISING REVENUE FOR FURTHER RESEARCH! THE MUSEUM OWES YOU *BOTH* A *GREAT DEBT!*

FREE COMIC BOOK ·DAY·

SATURDAY - MAY 7

www.freecomicbookday.com

ASK ABOUT YOUR FREE COMIC BOOK

At Participating Retailers Only

I GET IT! SOMEHOW THE SAFE FILTERS OUT MY SEE-THROUGH VISION! WHEN IT'S ON MY HEAD, I CAN'T SEE IT — BUT EVERYTHING ELSE LOOKS NORMAL!

WHAT? WHAT? IT'S NOT NORMAL! IT'S NUTS! AND IT'S ALL MY FAULT!

AW, IT'LL WEAR OFF SOON! BUT IN THE MEANTIME...

...I MIGHT AS WELL HAVE A LITTLE FUN WITH THIS!

C'MON!

AT MICKEY'S HOUSE ...

HOW DO YOU GIRLS LIKE MY SAFE NOW?

HUH? I DON'T GET IT?

HMM! LET ME TAKE A *PEEK!*

UH OH! I SEE A *HAIRLINE FRACTURE* ON THE SECOND BONE OF THE *BIG TOE!*

HA! SOME *JOKE*, MICKEY! YOU'RE AS BAD AS *KATY!*

RRRING!

EXCUSE ME, MICKEY!

OH, HELLO, *DR. BONES!*

HELLO, MINNIE! I'VE GOT YOUR *X-RAY!* YOUR LEG LOOKS *FINE...*

...EXCEPT FOR A *HAIRLINE FRACTURE* ON THE SECOND BONE OF THE *BIG TOE!*

HMPH! **VERRRY FUNNY!** NOW YOU'VE GOT DR. BONES PLAYING ALONG! WELL, I'VE HAD IT! **OUT!**

BUT...BUT...

SHEESH!

HI, GOOFY! IT'S ME — **MICKEY!**

HYUK! ALMOST DIDN'T RECOGNIZE YA, MICKEY! **NEW HAIRCUT?**

UH, **WELL**...

SAY, Y'AIN'T SEEN M' **KEYS,** HAVE YA?

HMM! LOOK IN YOUR **PANTS CUFF,** GOOFY!

GAWSH! Y'RE A DAD-BURNED **MIND-READER!**

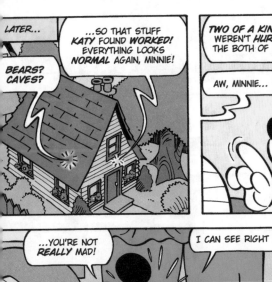

LATER...

...SO THAT STUFF *KATY* FOUND *WORKED!* EVERYTHING LOOKS *NORMAL* AGAIN, MINNIE!

BEARS? CAVES?

TWO OF A KIND! THANK GOODNESS YOU WEREN'T *HURT!* I OUGHT TO *SPANK* THE BOTH OF YOU!

AW, MINNIE...

...YOU'RE NOT *REALLY* MAD!

I CAN SEE RIGHT *THROUGH* YOU!

EH...NOT *LITERALLY,* OF COURSE! GULP!

HA HA HA HA

It Will Giv

YOU

X-RAY

VISION

![Scoop logo]

JEEPERS, CREEPERS, WHERE'D YOU GET THOSE PEEPERS?

Yes, one of the most coveted superpowers is now just a click away. Scoop opens your eyes to the latest ground-breaking news and lets you see beyond the surface of any new story - learn what the hottest new Batman statue is made of or find out the true origin of Wolverine. Crammed with powerful character images and the latest industry news, Scoop is the free weekly e-newletter from Gemstone Publishing and Diamond International Galleries that will give you the vision to toast your competition with your keen insider knowledge and product savvy. So, read Scoop and see your collection soar to the heights of Superman when you transform your collecting vision from 20/20 to 20/MONEY. Whether you're a pop culture enthusiast or a collecting fiend, visit http://scoop.diamondgalleries.com to check it all out and subscribe. No bones about it, Scoop is *ULTRAVIOLETLY FUN!!!*

THIS BETTER **WORK** — OR I'M TOAST!

YES! PERFECT!

SPROING!

THINGS ARE GOING **EXACTLY** AS PLANNED!

GOOD, GOOD! THE OLD **BOOT** IS WORKING JUST FINE...

...BUT MY REMOTE SUDDENLY **ISN'T!** WHAT'S UP?

APPARENTLY THE BATTERIES ARE LOW FROM THE **WORKOUT** THEY JUST GOT!

WELL NOW, LOOKS LIKE I'VE DUG UP QUITE A NUMBER OF *GLITCHES* IN THIS LATEST ROUND OF TESTING! IT'S *ALWAYS* THAT WAY WHEN I INSTALL A NEW SET OF MONEY BIN DEFENSES!

AND IT COULD BE WORSE! AT LEAST MR. McDUCK ISN'T UNDERFOOT!

WHILE HE'S DOWN IN LOWER KAWI-WAWI, NEGOTIATING AN EXPORT CONTRACT FOR THEIR FLYING WINGNUTS, I CAN STAMP OUT EVERY *BUG* I FIND!

THE NEW DEFENSES HAVE CHECKED OUT A-OK! NOW THE MACHINERY TAKES OVER WHILE WE *RELAX!*

MMMM!

MMMM!

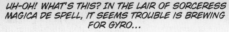

UH-OH! WHAT'S THIS? IN THE LAIR OF SORCERESS MAGICA DE SPELL, IT SEEMS TROUBLE IS BREWING FOR GYRO...

I NEED A VERY **STRONG** POTION!

EYE OF NEWT! HAIR OF DOG! WING OF BAT!

YES, THAT SHOULD DO NICELY!

PERFECT! BWAHAHA! **PERFECT!**

NOW TO PUT THIS POTENT STUFF TO ITS **PROPER** USE!

I'M TIP-TOP AND READY TO TAKE ON THE *WORLD* — SCROOGE McDUCK'S *MONEY BIN*, THAT IS! *HEE HEE!*

I'LL FINALLY GRAB HIS NUMBER ONE DIME WITH AN *ALL-OUT NO-HOLDS-BARRED ATTACK!*

NO HALF-BAKED SCHEMES THIS TIME! TODAY I REV UP MY SPELLCASTING TO A *FEVER* PITCH!

I'LL PREPARE POWERFUL POTIONS — *ONE* FOR *EACH* OBSTACLE THAT MIGHT COME UP, SO I'LL BE READY TO STOP AT *NOTHING...*

...UNTIL I *GET* WHAT I WANT!

IN THE MEANTIME, GYRO'S DEFENSES ARE ALL ON ALERT, LISTENING FOR ANYTHING LOUD AS A TRUCKHORSE OR QUIET AS A...

SQUEEK?

YAWN!

SO IS MAGICA PREPARING FOR NOTHING?

THAT'S THE *LAST* OF THE POTIONS!

NOTHING CAN STOP ME THIS TIME! I'M LOADED FOR BEAR...

...AND *ALSO* READY TO UTILIZE THE POWERS OF *SUBTLETY*!

GET OUT OF MY WAY, YOU STUPID GEESE! I'M IN *BUSINESS*!

HONK!

HONK! HONK!

IN BUSINESS, AND MORE POWERFUL THAN EVER BEFORE! BUT WHEN A DIRE THREAT LOOMS, HELP SOMETIMES COMES FROM A SOURCE...

HAHAHAHAHAHA! ARE YOU *READY* FOR ME, McDUCK?

'CAUSE READY OR *NOT*, HERE I COME!

...YOU'D LEAST EXPECT!

AAAOOGAH! AAAOOGAH!

THOSE WERE REAL ALARMS, BUT MY MONITORS DON'T *SHOW* AN INVASION! THERE MUST BE *SOMETHING* THERE...

...SO I'D BETTER..

H-HELLO!

OH, MY TWINKS AND SLATS! YOU–YOU'RE *ME!*

YES! AND I COME FROM A FUTURE WHERE MAGICA'S *BEATEN* YOU!

MAGICA?

MAGICA DE SPELL! SHE SET OFF YOUR ALARMS — YOU CAN'T SEE HER NOW BECAUSE SHE'S *INVISIBLE!*

IT'S NOON RIGHT NOW! IN AN HOUR SHE'LL HAVE *DEFEATED* YOU, TURNING YOU INTO ME!

YOU MEAN MY INVENTIONS *WON'T STOP* MAGICA?

THAT'S RIGHT! I CAME BACK TO *WARN* YOU BECAUSE...

...IF YOU'RE NOT *PREPARED* — YOU MIGHT NOT EVEN *SURVIVE* TO *BECOME* ME! BWAA-AAAH!

LISTEN, PAST SELF! I'M WARNING YOU TO *LOOK OUT!*

NOW, NOW! AS YOU SEE, MAGICA'S *LICKED!* EVERYTHING'S GOING TO BE FINE!

YOU ONLY *THINK* SHE IS! YOU'RE STILL GOING TO END UP AS *ME* AT ONE O' CLOCK!

SHE HAS A POTION FOR THIS! A POTION FOR THAT! SHE'S READY FOR *EVERY* ONE OF THE SECURITY MEASURES YOU'VE SET UP HERE!

SHE CAN'T BE STOPPED!

RELAX! THERE ARE LINES AND LINES AND LINES OF AUTOMATED DEFENSES! HOW CAN SHE BEAT THEM ALL?

NOT ONLY THAT, THERE ARE TRAPS DESIGNED FOR *JUST* THE LIKES OF HER! SHE DOESN'T STAND A CHANCE!

SIGH! I THOUGHT THE SAME WHEN I WAS YOU, THAT I HAD EVERYTHING COVERED! THEN MAGICA *TOOK OUT* MY TRAPS *ONE BY ONE!*

IT'S GOING TO BE *HORRIBLE!* SEE HOW I LOOK, PAST SELF — YOU'LL BARELY ESCAPE INTACT!

YOU'RE LOST — I MEAN *I'M* LOST! WE'RE *BOTH* LOST, YOU HEAR? *LOST!* THERE'S NO HOPE!

SO — *GULP!* — WHAT CAN WE DO *NOW* IF WE'VE *ALREADY* LOST IN THE FUTURE?

OUTSIDE...

CRACK!

HAH! NOTHING STOPS ME! I'M JUST GETTING *WARMED UP!*

THIS SHOULD HANDLE THE *NEXT* LITTLE PROBLEM!

NOW! ONCE *MORE* INTO THE BREACH!

YES! THIS IS GOING TO WORK NICELY...

...THERE'S NOTHING LIKE A VIAL OF *NO-GOODNESS* TO PUT THE *VERVE* BACK INTO MODERN LIFE!

SINS OF CIRCE, WHAT A MESS! *YEE-HEE-HEEE!*

ZAP!

ZAP!

AH, WELL...NO TIME TO ADMIRE MY HANDIWORK! I MUST BE GOING!

POOF!

HOORAY FOR OUR SIDE!

GREAT! BUT SO WHAT?!

SHE'LL JUST KEEP COMING AND COMING! DEFEATING EACH LINE OF DEFENSE AS SOON AS SHE *LEARNS* WHAT IT IS!

AT ONE-O-CLOCK YOU'LL *KNOW* THERE'S NO STOPPING HER! *SOB!* THEN YOU'LL BE *ME*!

OKAY, I GET THE MESSAGE! WHAT'S HAPPENED TO YOU — AND *WILL* HAPPEN TO *ME* — CAN'T BE CHANGED!

I'M IN FOR A PRETTY *ROUGH TIME*, LOOKS LIKE!

BUT PERHAPS MY DEFEAT DOESN'T HAVE TO BE *FINAL*...

GRRRRRR...

MROW?!

WOOF!

REEEOORR!

OKAY! AT ONE PM I'LL BE BEATEN! WHAT WAS — I MEAN, WHAT *WILL* IT BE LIKE?

AS I LAY THERE, DEFEATED AND STUNNED, I SAW HER *STEAL* MR. McDUCK'S NUMBER ONE DIME!

WHILE SHE WAS CROWING IN TRIUMPH, I CRAWLED AWAY!

I WAS BARELY ABLE TO *DRAG* MYSELF INTO MY TIME MACHINE AND COME BACK HERE TO WARN YOU!

GOOD THING YOU DID...

...'CAUSE I'LL NEED YOUR *HELP!*

MY HELP? TO DO WHAT? WHAT COULD WE POSSIBLY *DO?*

JUST THIS — *GET BACK* THAT NUMBER ONE DIME!

WE'LL OUTFOX MAGICA — MAYBE OUTFIGHT HER, TOO! TO THE TIME MACHINE!

WE'LL GO FORWARD TO ONE O' CLOCK AND SNATCH *VICTORY* FROM THE JAWS OF THIS IMPENDING DEFEAT!

BUT FIRST WE'LL GO TO *TWO* O' CLOCK — AND FIND OUT *HOW* TO DEFEAT MAGICA BY ASKING *YOUR* FUTURE SELF HOW HE'S *ALREADY DONE* IT!

EXCELLENT IDEA! THING IS...

...I DON'T REMEMBER HAVING *THOUGHT* OF IT BACK WHEN I WAS YOU!

IN FACT, DO I EVEN RECALL MEETING *ME* WHEN I WAS YOU? OH, WELL — *GULP!* — NOTHING VENTURED, I GUESS...

FORWARD...

TO BE SAFE, I SET THE CONTROLS TO TAKE US *OUT* OF THE BIN DURING OUR TIME-HOP!

LOOK! MAGICA BLASTED OPEN THAT DOOR — *NOW* IT'S OKAY AGAIN! WHAT GIVES?

WE'RE IN A FUTURE WHERE MAGICA'S BEEN BEATEN, THAT'S WHAT! AFTER THAT, OUR FUTURE SELF *FIXED* ALL THE STUFF THAT WAS DAMAGED!

"AND IF I'M RIGHT ABOUT ALL THIS, HE'S PROBABLY EXPECTING US TO SHOW UP ABOUT NOW!"

HIYA! BET YOU'RE HERE TO FIND OUT HOW TO *DEFEAT* MAGICA, EH?

DONUTS

DONUTS

DONUTS

BELIEVE IT OR NOT, IT COMES DOWN TO HAVING A LARGE SUPPLY OF *DONUTS!* I'D EXPLAIN WHY, BUT IT'S BETTER YOU FOUND OUT FOR YOURSELVES!

DONUTS

DONUTS

I GUESS WE SHOULD TRUST HIM, HUH!

WE'D BE FOOLISH *NOT* TO! WHATEVER HE DID, IT MUST DO THE TRICK!

I ALMOST FORGOT! YOU'LL NEED ONE *MORE* THING...

...*THIS!*

SHORTLY...

OKAY! THAT'S THE LAST OF THE LOT!

LET'S GET THIS GIZMO ONTO THE SPACE-TIME CONTINUUM...

...AND CRUISE BACK TO *ONE O'CLOCK* AND MAGICA'S *VICTORY!*

SIGH! MY **DEFEAT**...

DEFEAT, **NOTHING!** WE'RE GOING TO **FOLLOW** MAGICA NOW...

...AND CATCH UP WITH HER AT HER **LAIR!**

UH — SURE! WHY DON'T **I** THINK OF THESE THINGS?

HAHAHAHAHAHA!

I DON'T GET IT, PAST SELF! YOU KEEP COMING UP WITH IDEAS THAT **I** DON'T REMEMBER HAVING! IT'S WEIRD!

I GUESS IT'S NO BIG DEAL THOUGH, HUH?

HAH! IN MOMENTS, I'LL BE THE MOST **POWERFUL** WOMAN ON EARTH!

ONWARD! *GULP!* OR ARE WE ACTING *RASHLY?*

I'LL TRUST OUR FUTURE SELF! HE *DID* SORT OF HINT THIS WOULD WORK OUT OKAY!

OKAY! STEADY — LOAD IN THE DONUTS AND PREPARE TO FIRE!

RIGHT!

OKAY, DIME, YOU'RE ABOUT TO BECOME A *MAGIC WEALTH AMULET!*

HEY!

FOONT!

YOU MEDDLERS! PREPARE TO SPEND THE REST OF YOUR LIVES AS *CHICKENS!*

ULP!

LOOK! IF WE CAN GET *THOSE*, WE STAND A FIGHTING CHANCE TO *REALLY* DEFEAT HER – FOR GOOD!

I'LL GET 'EM! HANG ON!

HOW DO WE KNOW WHAT EACH ONE DOES?

WE *DON'T!* AT THIS POINT WE'LL JUST TAKE POT LUCK!

GASP!

EEEP!

SMASH!

ONE MORE TIME — I'M *YOUR FUTURE SELF!* WHEN YOU THINK OF THINGS, I SHOULD *REMEMBER* HAVING THOUGHT OF THEM MYSELF!

BUT NO — YOU'RE GETTING IDEAS I *CAN'T* RECALL! YOU'RE LEADING YOUR LIFE DOWN A *NEW PATH...*

AND *CHANGING* THE COURSE OF EVENTS?

SEEMS LIKE IT! WHAT IF YOU CHANGE THE FUTURE SO *YOU NEVER BECOME ME*? MAYBE ONE OF US WOULD *DISAPPEAR!*

OR *BOTH* OF US! OR THE *WORLD* AS WE KNOW IT!

ULP!

NO TIME TO LOSE! LET'S *WRECK* MAGICA'S LAB, THEN SEE ABOUT SETTING THINGS *RIGHT!*

WE NEED TO DESTROY *ALL* HER VIALS — MAKE HER THINK TWICE ABOUT COMING AFTER US AFTER HER FROG POTION WEARS OFF!

WE'RE BETTER OFF *NOT KNOWING* WHAT MISCHIEF WE'VE PREVENTED!

NEXT WE'LL FIX THE TIME CONTINUUM!

GOOD OL' NUMBER ONE! SILLY MAGICA SEES IT AS A MAGIC CHARM, EVEN THOUGH MR. McDUCK ONLY KEEPS IT BECAUSE...

HEY! *LOOK OUT!*

YOO HOO!

SNAP! SNAP!

HMM...MY PAST SELF SEEMS OKAY, BUT HE'S COMPLETELY *OUT* OF IT...

...AND I THINK I *KNOW* WHAT HAPPENED!

AMNESIA POTION

DISORIENTATION COUPLED TO SHORT-TERM MEMORY LOSS! *OF COURSE!*

HERE'S WHY I DON'T RECALL MY PAST SELF'S EXPERIENCES! HE *FORGETS* THEM BEFORE *BECOMING* ME!

I'LL TAKE HIM BACK TO JUST BEFORE ONE O'CLOCK! WHEN HE COMES TO HIS SENSES HE'LL THINK HE *NEVER LEFT*...

$

...AND MAGICA WILL DEFEAT HIM, TURNING HIM INTO ME *RIGHT ON SCHEDULE!*

ASSURED THAT THE COURSE OF EVENTS HASN'T BEEN CHANGED, THE FUTURE GYRO — NOW THE PRESENT GYRO — TRAVELS FORWARD TO 1:30! HE REPAIRS THE DAMAGE INFLICTED BY MAGICA ON THE MONEY BIN...

THERE NOW! EVERYTHING'S SHIPSHAPE AGAIN!

PERFECT! NOW I JUST FETCH A BIG LOAD OF *DONUTS* AND A TENNIS-BALL-SERVING MACHINE, GET THEM ALL HERE BY TWO O'CLOCK...

...AND I'LL BE ALL SET FOR MY PAST SELVES TO ARRIVE!

I DO ADMIT A *FONDNESS* FOR THESE — CHOCOLATE-GLAZED, ESPECIALLY!